Shakespeare's Avon from source to Severn
by Richard Shurey

The river at Strensham.

Shakespeare's Avon from Source to Severn

by Richard Shurey

Following the footsteps of traveller-extraordinary
Charles Showell, whose drawings of 1900 are compared
with the same scenes today, photographed by the
author.

The Whitethorn Press

Published by
The Whitethorn Press Limited
Thomson House Withy Grove Manchester M60 4BL

Litho preparation and phototypeset in Plantin 110
by Lapex Graphics Limited Heswall
Printed in England by Carrprint (Manchester) Limited
Barnoldswick

ISBN 0 9506055 9 X

Illustrations

Naseby.

Stratford-upon-Avon.

Bredon.

Nafford Mill

8

INTRODUCTION

AT the turn of the century, Charles Showell wrote a delightful record of a jaunt he made down Shakespeare's Avon. He travelled from the river's humble source near the historic Civil War battle site at Naseby on the borders of Northamptonshire and Leicestershire, to the confluence with the Severn at another famous place of conflict, Tewkesbury.

For many years, I have walked beside this meandering waterway, and have often thought how fascinating it would be to repeat Showell's journey along its entire tranquil route. His book contains many of his pen and ink drawings, and these portray the scenery of those distant years as vividly as any photographic record. They enable a unique comparison to be made with the villages, towns and countryside of today, and I have achieved this by photographs which are, as near as possible, exact matches of Showell's drawings. So come with me as I trace the river through the very heart of England, past massive castles, humble and picturesque hamlets, watermills and ancient towns which reflect the history of our land. I have used definitive rights of way or other recognised pathways such as canal tow-paths to keep as near as possible to the river or to follow Showell's route when he strayed away to visit interesting places nearby. Wherever I could, like Showell, I avoided main highways.

RICHARD SHUREY

Nafford Mill near Pershore.

9

Dedicated to Rosemary

Author's note
Charles Showell was a director at the turn of the century of the Birmingham firm of brassfounders, Edwin Showell & Sons Ltd. He was a noted artist specialising in fine watercolours, and was president of the Royal Birmingham Society of Artists and also of St. Paul's Club, Birmingham.

I would like to express my appreciation of the kind co-operation of Mr. Donald Showell and Mr. Geoffrey D. Showell, grandsons of Charles Showell, over the publication of this book.

The source; the walk begins

Naseby was described by Showell as being "a very dead alive sort of place – it has lost much of its old world appearance, Lord Clifden having, of late years, built a number of superior cottages, the front gardens of which are adorned with fine Irish yews; these, however, give the main street quite a funereal aspect". (These workers' cottages had received the commendation of the Royal Commission of Labour a few years earlier, in 1892, when they were described as "well appointed in all aspects").

Our traveller quotes from a work by the Reverend John Mastin, who was curate of Naseby from 1778 to 1783 and subsequently incumbent of the parish until 1829. Mastin's *The History and Antiquities of Naseby in the County of Northampton* was written at the end of the eighteenth century, just before the act of enclosure for Naseby was passed in 1820.

Mastin wanted to put the then very remote Naseby on the map and, to the great benefit of later historians, not only described the epic Civil War battle but also gave a lively and detailed account of the village at that time.

The buildings, in Mastin's day, were almost all cob cottages and roofed in thatch. The exceptions were the church, the vicarage, Shuckburgh House and the manor house. The cob cottages were built of Kealy earth, "dug close by, excellent in its kind and the best calculated for building I ever saw. Walls built of this earth are exceedingly strong and, if kept dry, said to be more durable than if built of soft stone or indifferent bricks. There are walls built of this earth in some of the houses said to be two hundred years old and, were they washed over with lime water, their appearance would be respectable; but, instead of this, the new coat, which they have once a year, consists of cow dung, spread upon them to dry for firing".

The Kealy houses were still much in evidence when Showell made his journey a hundred years after Mastin's description, but the Fitzgerald Arms had been reconstructed to replace the earlier cob and thatch Bell Inn.

Today, the commended brick cottages remain, but there are no Kealy earth houses or walls. Until recent years, the village population gradually declined from the 600 of Mastin's time to less than 500 after the agricultural depression at the end of the century, and to 350 in 1951. The construction of new dwellings for commuters has reversed the trend, but it is conjectural as to how long this will continue, with the rising cost of travel.

The church site is very old, with records dating back to 1228. The spire has only been a landmark since its construction in 1860, when it cost £350, including the building of the tower.

Mastin recorded that the earlier tower could be climbed. "A most extensive view in all directions is obtained; with a good glass from the top can be seen Boston Deeps on an arm of the sea in Lincolnshire, distance nearly sixty miles north-east; also, as many as forty parish churches".

Showell was not impressed with the church building – "Not at all a picturesque edifice, saving the porch".

The copper ball, which used to top the low tower, was thought to have been looted and brought from Boulogne in 1544, by Sir Gyles Allington. The sphere decorated his house at Horseheath, in Cambridgeshire, but was purchased by George Ashby, the

The site of the Battle of Naseby. In 1645, the final and decisive event of the Civil War was enacted on these flat lands.

patron of the living, for its weight as old copper. When the ball became superfluous with the completion of the spire, it was placed on a plinth outside the church door, where it remains today.

The site of the great battle of 1645 is some three-quarters of a mile from the village. The event was the final and decisive encounter of the Civil War and, at the end of the day, the Parliamentarians and Cromwell triumphed, Charles I lost his crown and five thousand men lost their lives.

The day-long struggle seems to have had little effect on the lives of the locals, there being no account of the fighting in parish or other local records. The ubiquitous Reverend Mastin noted that he found one old villager who could remember a Naseby man recalling the battle with folk "coming from all quarters" to help bury the dead on the battlefield.

Relics of the fight have been unearthed by the plough over the centuries. Showell said that a farmer offered him two recently-found bullets. The countryman "was uncertain as to the present market value of bullets, some visitors giving as much as half-a-crown each. Assuring him that that was altogether too sublime a figure for me, he benevolently dropped the price to a shilling, which I accepted". Showell then offered to send him over from Birmingham a quantity of new bullets at twopence a pound adding that "doubtless bullets will be available for future ages". A museum has recently been established in the village where, no doubt, the genuine items only will be displayed!

In more recent times, the initial skirmishes of what has been called the "Second Battle of Naseby" have been fought. These have resulted from proposals to place a motorway near the village, one route of which would destroy, for all time, the ancient battlefield. Today, one can visit the isolated Cromwell monument, which is set in pastoral lands, close one's eyes and perhaps hear the clash of sword and sound of musket, and sniff the odour of powder. Let us hope that, for future generations, this will not be replaced by the more realistic roar of passing motors and the stench of engine fumes.

The actual source of the Avon is a well, now situated in the garden of Manor Farm opposite Naseby Church. The spot is 600 feet above sea level (which, incidentally,

Naseby: the waters of Shakespeare's Avon first flow from a spring opposite the church.

Welford-on-Avon, one of two villages bearing this name on the river's course. After five meandering miles, this is where the river meets its first road.

makes the place the second highest village in the county. It is also interesting to note that the River Nene rises only a mile away, the waters of which flow in the opposite direction to those of the Avon, to arrive eventually at the North Sea).

From the inauspicious spring, the Avon is culverted under the road and through the cellars of the Fitzgerald Arms. (The Fitzgeralds became lords of the manor at the time of enclosure). Showell tells us that once the infant river flowed through the bill of a plaster swan and into an ornamental pool. "But alas!" he writes, "There were, as indeed there are at most places, urchins at Naseby. The sight of a swan constantly on tap was too much for them and it was soon demolished". Vandalism is indeed timeless.

Mastin tells us that the locals in 1800 had "a kind of provincial dialect and, in general, vociferate loudly". Showell, a hundred years on, found that the landlady of the Fitzgerald Arms spoke similarly when he was told he could have some "tay and chaaze". Today the inn is a headquarters of the Sealed Knot Society which periodically re-enacts battles of the Civil War to bring excitement and colour to many a fête and other functions.

The river is little more than a ditch on emerging from the depths and, to reach its course again, I turned down Carvel's Lane.

Nearby is the Wesley Methodist Chapel, erected in 1825. This place of worship is a reminder of the strong non-conformist zeal of the last century. In the year before it was built, a letter was sent to John Fitzgerald asking for a piece of land to build the chapel. The structure would be "the means of promoting the temporal and spiritual welfare of many of the inhabitants of this populous village". Among the forty-one signatories, there were the names of fourteen of the twenty farmers of the parish.

Carvel's Lane used to be called Coal Pits Lane and was one of several constructed straight across the flat farmland by the Enclosure Commissioners. To surface these roads, they opened four stone, chalk, rubble and gravel pits, and at the same time, decreed that three drains should be dug. This involved the straightening of the streams contributing to the River Avon.

The river is crossed without one being aware of the fact, but when it emerges from the reservoir of the Grand Union Canal, it has gained some power, as though joyful and eager to be wending its way through the green landscape.

The A50 is a busy road so I soon turned down the driveway to Welford Lodge. Below this, nudging up to the Avon, is another farm, Sulby Abbey. This was where the ancient abbey was founded in 1155 by William de Wyvile, Lord of Welford.

The stately looking farmhouse was abandoned because of severe dry rot. The last occupants moved a few years ago to a less romantic but, no doubt more comfortable residence, high on the lane. Showell reported that, a few years earlier than his walk, Lady Villiers, owner of the land, built a chamber for the reception of relics dug up from time to time. It then contained a stone slab from the tomb of a church dignitary, a stone coffin and what looked like a child's coffin.

The present farmer of these lands has dug up more items dating from the days of the abbey, and they have been added to the collection of Lady Villiers.

The infant river winds a devious way through lush meadows to Welford – the first of two places so named on the Avon. Charles Showell did not find this Welford an attractive village, "being built mainly of brick and lying on a gentle slope to the east; its tameness, however, is slightly redeemed by a few Kealy earth-built cottages".

Adjacent to the church is a fine manor house with a large wall sundial reminding us that *hora pars vitae.*

And so back to the Avon. Showell sketched the first road bridge of the river, with the castellated George Inn in the background. Here, he slaked his thirst at the hostelry "whose host rejoices in the patronymic of W. S. Gilbert but disclaims any connection with the other celebrated character of that name''. Showell's drawing could well have been executed yesterday.

Alongside the inn is a branch terminus of the Grand Union Canal, where the warehouses are now used as a depot for craft holiday-cruising on the waterway. I enquired of a mechanic about the change of name of the inn to Wharf House Hotel and was advised to ask a Miss Gilbert who lived in a cottage overlooking the canal.

Miss Gilbert was a lively lady in her eighties. Sitting in the sunshine, she enthusiastically reminisced about the time at the turn of the century when her father was landlord of the George. The name was altered when the place was purchased in about 1960 by a brewery concern. She is still proud to share the name of the famous W. S. Gilbert, and to point out that the holiday boats are all named after Gilbert and Sullivan characters. So Lady Blanche was tied to Princess Ida, and Craythorne daringly rubbed shoulders with Nanki Poo and Tit Willow.

Alongside the feeder canal from Welford, the Avon demurely hides herself among the thick reeds as if hesitant of which route to take. As I walked, the only sound was of a huntsman's horn and the only movement was the silent flitting of a wren in the hedgerow.

This is an unspectacular valley but nevertheless picturesque and gentle. The balance bridges of Showell's day are no more or remain decaying and broken, replaced by utilitarian and harsh rigid structures. But Bosworth Mill, the first on the river, resolutely remains and is being painstakingly renovated. Unfortunately the water-wheel is missing, but an old steam engine, similar to the former stand-by machine, is to be used again to set the mill into motion once more.

When the Welford branch joins the main Grand Union Canal, we obtain another glimpse of the shy Avon as it emerges from a tunnel below the waterway. The valley is now broad with the smoothed uplands intensely farmed.

Leaving the tow-path, I crossed an elegant wrought-iron bridge which once spanned the tracks of the Rugby and Stamford branch of the London and North-Western Railway (alas, the line is no more) to arrive at Kilworth Mill. The structure to the right in Showell's sketch was demolished in 1947, but the rest of the mill is little changed. The

Bosworth Mill, the first mill on the Avon, still resolutely remains.

*Kilworth Mill Farm. The lonely miller's house is empty and the mill
has long passed into history.*

Stanford Church, virtually unchanged since the turn of the century.

only evidence of the former activities is a grinding-wheel now used as a step in the kitchen.

This corner of Leicestershire is part of the northern territory of the Pytchley Hunt – the areas of the hunts have little regard for county boundaries. The farmers at Kilworth Mill would certainly have welcomed the continuing tradition of the sport, as foxes have been as much of a problem as they ever were.

From the mill, there is a climb out of the vale along a bridleway to North Kilworth. The approach to the spired church of St. Andrew is most attractive and the cows in the surrounding meadows were as impassive as Showell found them, as though mildly surprised that anyone should pass this way.

North Kilworth's twin village, South Kilworth, looked neat and trim, although a prominent notice warned offenders of "an unprecedented amount of litter". But the place looked alive with crowded inns, in which space could still be found for old-fashioned bar games.

Beyond the Kilworths, the Avon has been dammed to form a vast reservoir. The general public can only look from afar as this is a drinking water supply; but to the flocks of Canada geese it is a home.

By an elaborate signpost, where one is informed that the distance to Bitteswell, through Willoughby Waterless, is $16\frac{1}{2}$ miles, I turned left along Stanford Road. This is a charming avenue of beech trees, as beautiful today as at the turn of the century. Like Showell, I too journeyed to these parts on a sunny day in early November. He remarked on the first glimpse of the Hall of Stanford, and on how he found ". . . the effect of sunlight, broad shadows and autumnal tints, was truly enchanting".

The river (it now merits the name, at last), is crossed by a new bridge of unweathered and unromantic brick, to take the traveller into Northamptonshire again and to Stanford Church.

This church, with a solid, squat tower, is a fourteenth-century gem, although now little used for regular worship. There are many elaborate tombs and monuments to the Verneys, Otways and Brayes; and carvings of a fine precision, with glass, colourful and rare. These are treasures, indeed, which one hopes will be preserved.

Showell had little to report on the length of the Avon from Stanford to Rugby, but I was left with the impression that this is the stretch when the river, like a child starlet of the nineteen-thirties screen epics, at last assumes the status of an adult with great reluctance. Up to now, the languid waterway has been floundering with little purpose and almost getting lost in reeds and marshland at times. At the end of this day's walk, the Avon was a genuine river, with character and depth, and with pools and fish and anglers.

It also experiences its first real encounter with the modern world, where the gentle noise of running water now merges with the constant drone of traffic on the M1 motorway.

The Braye family of Stanford Hall now share their home with a motor museum and there was the din of hydroplane racing in the grounds. But the avenue of fine trees and a footpath across the field to Swinford are pleasant enough. Showell noted the old flags and boards in the hedgerows to warn the riders in the hunt that the country is "cursed with wire". Today it is the rambler who is for ever complaining of wire across rights of way.

Swinford had "a few picturesque bits, including the church tower in a most delightful state of dilapidation". To its credit, the village must have put some work into the church; with stones of many hues it is now safe for many more years, and the clock we are told "was installed as a memorial to those who died in the 1939-45 war".

"A pleasant walk of about two miles," Showell tells us, "brings the traveller to Catthorpe". Alas those days are no more.

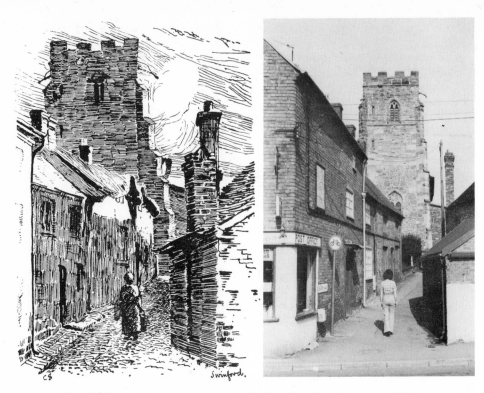

Swinford – a picturesque corner, including the church tower, which in 1900 was in "a most delightful state of dilapidation".

The modern bridge carrying the A5 highway leap-frogs the ancient Dow Bridge of 1232.

The footpath out of the village took me over fields where the habitat of nature had been sacrificed to the stubble-burning flames in the name of efficient farming. The huge flock of lapwings did not seem to mind, but the ridge on which the motorway is perched was the backcloth, and I found the prospect barren, treeless and depressing.

A motorway sign announces in huge letters that this is (or was a mile or so back) the River Avon. I doubt whether many drivers really care that the humble strip of marshland below contains the tender child of Shakespeare's river.

My deflated spirits were not raised by Catthorpe which "once boasted of a poet-parson named Dyer who, having tried his hand at painting and versifying, ultimately found himself vicar in the year 1741". Today, he would find difficulty in constructing a tranquil rhyme. Catthorpe is an island in the middle of a sea of main roads.

Day and night, the drone of vehicles is constant; the village no doubt had learned to live with the A5 – Watling Street – since the Roman soldiers tramped from Canterbury to Chester, but throw in the M1 and M6, and travellers have now dealt a cruel and excessive blow to Catthorpe.

Watling Street is crossed at Dow or Dove Bridge. The parapets, dated 1232, are narrow and the arches low, but this structure has now been gracefully retired and is replaced by a utilitarian if less attractive single span. So here we cross the Avon, the Roman highway and the border into Warwickshire.

The path to Clifton-on-Dunsmore is along an ancient green road – a track which the drovers used but the modern road-maker spurned. For a few yards, the way is bordered by a discreet railway embankment which has been used as a dam to create pools for fish breeding. The din of the motor car now recedes, and the sounds are of nature, and the movement is of rabbits darting for safety or a colourful kingfisher skimming over the river.

Showell reminds us that Clifton was owned at the time of Edward the Confessor by Alwine Alwinas, ancestor of the Arden family. (It will be remembered that Shakespeare's mother was an Arden).

Clifton was once a place of some importance. The present parish church of Rugby was, as far back as 1140, a chapel of ease of the mother-church of Clifton.

One of the sons of Clifton was Lawrence Sheriff, who died in 1567. He became a wealthy grocer in London and left funds for the founding of a grammar school in Rugby which was to become the famous public school.

The church has a carving on a wall of a muzzled bear. The animal was the badge of the Barefoot family and its display on the tower is the explanation of a couplet referring to the church and the Old Lion Inn which stood where we now see the village hall:

Ye younge men of Cliftone of ye Lion beware
If ye wish to be happy, turn in at ye Bayre.

The river is met again along a lane where lovers over the ages have pledged their love on the bridge across an abandoned arm of a canal. Nearby, is Clifton Mill, little changed over the years, while the river now commands respect passing through a wide flood plain frequented by fishermen. But Brownsover Mill is long departed and replaced by a couple of garages alongside a reservoir of the Oxford Canal.

So the Avon skirts Rugby, which was described by Showell as a town of almost abnormal growth. It is still growing, with extensive housing estates bulging into the countryside north of the river, and tower blocks of flats. But as Showell says, although rather nondescript, the town is of some antiquity, and dates back to the time of the Saxons. At Domesday, it appears as Rocheberrie, but the castle was demolished during the reign of Henry II.

"It stands on rising ground between which and the Ural Mountains, there is nothing

21

Little Lawford Mill, mentioned in the Domesday Book, still withstands the waters of the Avon.

to intercept the wind". So said Dr. Arnold, the one-time headmaster of Rugby School; and who that has heard of Rugby has not heard of Dr. Arnold – or of one of our great poets, Rupert Brooke? At 5 Hillmorton Road in Rugby is a plaque proclaiming: "In this house was born R. Brooke, 1887".

The river is met by the waters of another stream – the Swift – then slips between vast industrial complexes to emerge fairly unscathed at Newbold-on-Avon. This place belonged to Geffry Wirce in the Conqueror's day, who "for his health (I suppose, of his soul), granted the greater part of the tithes to the monks of Kirby". When Elizabeth I was Queen, the lord of the manor was one St. Thomas Leigh Kt., who lived further down the Avon at Stoneleigh, and was to become an Alderman of London.

The church at Newbold-on-Avon is dedicated to St. Botolph, appropriately for us, the patron saint of travellers. Showell despaired about the village's close proximity to Rugby, but it has, for the great part, resisted being swallowed by its big brother neighbour.

The open countryside of a lovely valley is beyond the church. The path over a stile descends to an arm of the Oxford Canal to the north of the church. The arm was built in the middle of the last century, twisting about in an aimless sort of fashion, and terminating abruptly in a tunnel nearby and never coming out the other end. It used to be a saying at Newbold "that the bargee could hear Newbold church clock strike all twenty-four hours", because of the time taken to pass the place.

Now the canal feeder is only for nature, and she has made good use of the moisture laden clays; vegetation is lush and birds flit among the tall reeds. A long and substantial bridge has been built to take the walker over the flood plain of the river.

Little Lawford Mill is still fairly intact; a bridge conveys the bridleway over the water but the motorist must use the ford.

The saline springs of Newnham Regis along the lane to Kings Newnham are for ever gone. Not that they were ever much it would seem. The connection with royalty implied in the name came from the springs' ownership by the crown from Edward I to Edward VI. An attempt was made to construct a rival town to Leamington Spa, but plans came to naught; it never got beyond the pegging out stage.

Showell tells of a medical man of repute, a Mr. Bailey, M.D., who wrote a pamphlet on the proposed spa's virtues: "I do not know if he was rewarded at the same rate of payment as the modern penny-a-liner, or whether he was promised so many paid-up shares in the new venture, as would have been the case in the year 1898".

The pamphlet enumerated the various maladies for which the spa treatment was an antidote, and cautioned against the abuse of the waters. After dwelling on the fact "that the learned do dispute whether such waters should be taken or not in the leap year", he advises he "would not rashly counsel any to use them in leap year unless great cause do urge them. As for the quantity, I have known some to have drunken 10 pints in a morning and some 12, but for my part, I cannot in any wise either commend or like of these excessive quantities".

Ireland, a chronicler of 1795, tells that the springs were much frequented, "and would probably be much more so were the roads kept in a passable state".

But the road is no trouble today. It's as delightful an English lane as one could see, through a pastoral countryside to Kings Newnham. Here a well-used footpath descends steeply by the garden of a new bungalow to the site of Newnham Mill. The substantial bridge over which Showell walked can still be seen, but all that remains of the mill building is a wall of brick; the great wooden spindle now slowly rots in the mud and weed. We must go on, therefore, to the church we can see on the hill.

The Church of St. Peter at Church Lawford has thirteenth-century work in the fabric, but the ardent restorers of a hundred years ago have left their mark. Showell

Above and right *Newnham Mill: the great wooden spindle now slowly rots in the mud and weed.*

Church Lawford, seen across the green vale of the upper Avon.

called at the Blue Lion Inn and remarked on the sign of the noble beast "with a most prodigious tail, exactly resembling a mooring line thrown from a ship". The inn has changed both its colour and family, and is now the White Lion.

The landlord showed me the prospectus when the estate was split up and sold, only a few years after Showell called, and it was then that the name of the hostelry was altered. The village stocks can no longer be seen on the green through the window; perhaps they too disappeared into past history with the Blue Lion.

In a hesitant fashion the river travels due west for a mile or so to Bretford. Overlooking the valley is the tower of what was once St. Lawrence's Church, now residing in a farmyard. Eighty years ago the structure was without a roof and surrounded by scaffolding. Showell remarked: "All honour to the Duke of Buccleuch" for the repairs which were in hand in 1900. The Duke's men obviously did him proud. The roof is still secure and we echo Showell's words that "long may it remain so".

Geoffry de Clinton founded a cell for nuns at Bretford (otherwise Bradforde or

The former stocks at Church Lawford.

Overlooking the river valley near Bretford is the tower of what was once St. Lawrence's Church, now residing in a farmyard.

26

Broadford). The village lies on the great Roman Way called the Fosse, and Geoffry's descendant, Theobald, had a gallows installed here.

Showell reminds us that the possession of a gallows, with an assize of bread and beer, appears to have been a privilege much prized by the aristocracy of those days, probably as a good investment.

At the turn of the century, the Roman highway was carried over the Avon by a "fine stone bridge". Now the old arches cannot cope with the heavy traffic, and impatient motorists are held up by traffic lights. Showell said Bretford looked extremely poverty-stricken; some cottages may still look humble with leaning walls and dipping roofs, but these places are now sought after by affluent folk escaping from the box world of housing estates. Add bow windows and a bottle glass or two, and a building is transformed; there are tubs of geraniums outside the white painted Queen's Head, and hanging baskets too. No, it's not at all a bad place now.

I took the farm track by the river which passes Marston Mill – Showell called it

Marston Mill has gone but the miller's house remains.

Wolston still has the Red Lion, but it has lost its old Manor House.

28

Mersdon. The miller's house still remains, but the old mill has gone.

The Avon and main Rugby-Coventry railway divide the two villages of Brandon and Wolston, the former on the high ground, the other at river level. Showell contrasted them thus: "Brandon has no church but is a bright, clean, happy and prosperous-looking village, with a workingmen's club and institute. Wolston is a large village, has a very fine interesting old church, yet it is a cheerless, thriftless-looking place, where apparently nothing is done to brighten the lives of its people."

Today, the division is different; Brandon has retained its small, closely-knit community; the club prospers still and the local folk seem to know each other. Wolston has lost its Old Manor House, but it has gained spruceness, tidy flower beds and lawns and hundreds of newcomers. But it has lost a rural characteristic of modest simplicity.

Entering Wolston, we go by the Priory – of uncertain age (perhaps about 1640) and probably a cell of nearby Coombe Abbey.

The Wilcox family provided the squire when Showell was here, and I noticed they were the patrons of the living of the church for many years until 1926.

The destruction of Wolston Mill is complete; the fallen masonry is covered with lush nettles surrounded by tall trees. There is now only birdsong in this tranquil spot where once was the bustle and movement of a working watermill.

Showell was recommended by a millhand to follow the banks of the river. "But he did not communicate to me the fact that I could easily have lost myself in the labyrinth of twisting river, back-water and bogs". I, therefore, stuck to the public ways – but with blocked pathways, barbed wire of Colditz proportions and high brambles, I doubt if my route was any easier than Showell's.

I climbed the hill to Ryton-on-Dunsmore, a village by the busy A45 trunk road. The history is old; Rieton-super-Dunsmore was given by Earl Leofric (husband of Lady Godiva) to the Priory of Coventry in 1043. "Poor Ryton Church!" lamented Showell. "The church has suffered many vicissitudes, as it does not fail to tell the beholder; it has been bandied about from spiritual to temporal powers and vice versa."

The porch of brick still covers the early Norman doorway and there is a neatness about the approach to the church. Showell also complained, a little churlishly, about the Norman windows being replaced by those of the fourteenth century; a lively building is in a continuous state of change. A corrugated iron hut which Showell bemoaned, is now the site of a handsome youth centre in an attractive, albeit modern, style. Beyond the church and across the A45 racetrack, are the giant Talbot works.

The old heathland of Dunsmore Heath is now largely under the plough and we are reminded that it was, in times past, a desolate wilderness on which people have been known to lose their way and even to perish.

Showell called the mill of Ryton "uninteresting", but I started off with a determined mind to seek out the place. After turning off the highway, I was confronted with notices reading "Private Road" and "Alsatian dogs on guard", so I hastened the next half-mile to Ryton Bridge.

The bridge is now a hybrid affair. To satisfy the insatiable demands of the motor car, two recent bridges have been tacked on to the original arches, so the river is funnelled through a long tunnel; the water chases through at a considerable pace, as though anxious to reach the daylight again.

I took the direction indicated by a footpath sign along the bankside. The track is clear and well used by anglers. Unfortunately, they have left their visiting cards, with sandwich bags and beer cans in abundance.

Bubbenhall, which at one time belonged to Sir John Beauchamp who was hanged, drawn and quartered, has the usual new houses attached to the old hub; but here the additions have been sited and built with discretion. Pride is the essential ingredient

Stoneleigh Abbey. Today, many acres of the estate accommodate the buildings of the National Agricultural Centre, home of the Royal Show.

which makes the place so finely attractive, but, sadly, the church of St. Giles, like so many others with treasures, has to be kept locked to keep out the vandals.

The building has obviously changed little in the years of this century. We can still see the little porch of wood bearing the date 1616 (but the woodworm is doing its utmost to eat the date away). The footpath from the churchyard and by the riverside is shaded and charming, but the mill site is now occupied by an elegant and expensive mansion. My quest for the old mills of Avon was singularly unlucky on this particular day.

Over Cloud Bridge (Clude = Saxon rock), a couple of miles or so further on, is a lane leading to Stoneleigh. As Showell said, "it's an English one!" And he added: "I will venture to say there is not a more romantic one in all Warwickshire, and that is saying, not in the whole world. It is a wonderfully green lane, edged . . . by the rugged oak fence usually found bordering a deer park. Trees of all kinds in wild luxuriance; no signs of life save that of birds in their branches, and the squirrel darting across the road". So, with a sprightly step I too neared Stoneleigh.

Stoneleigh – very pretty the village looked to Showell – and very pretty it still looks today. Remarkably, time seems to have given this place a miss – once you get off the main road and to the seclusion of the green.

The blacksmith still does a steady shoeing trade under the spreading leafy tree, and alongside the green are almshouses. In 1558, Alice, wife of Sir Thomas Leigh, Lord Mayor of London, built ten dwellings for five men and five women, unmarried. They had their full complement of tenants seventy-five years ago, but today, the old folk do not have to be single to live in these houses of weathered stone.

Before the Normans came, Stoneleigh was held by King Edward. William the Conqueror liked it too, and it remained in the hands of royalty until the time of Henry II who had a house in the village.

Along Church Lane is the massive edifice of the village church of Mary the Virgin. It has many magnificent features but perhaps the finest is the chancel with its elaborate zig-zag carvings.

A mile away, in the year 1154, the monks of the Cistercian Order built their abbey on the banks of the Avon. Showell reminds us that in due time this place became a house of indulgence for idle men – "by no means an uncommon state of affairs" – and ultimately the site of the present classical residence.

Much of the old abbey perished in a fire in 1245 and King Henry III allowed the monks "fourty oaks out of his woods at Kenilworth for its reconstruction". The present gate-house and the church were extensively remodelled by Abbot Robert de Hockele when the living was granted to the monastery of Kenilworth during the first half of the twelfth century.

"One cannot stand at the gate-house and call to mind past history," wrote Showell, "without cursing the memory of Henry VIII, not so much for robbing the abbeys of their wealth – much of it ill-gotten gain and ill-spent – but for causing too many noble examples of beautiful architecture to be lost to the world for ever. Apparently, after he had taken their treasures, cash and lands, anybody could have these gems to despoil and convert into rubbish heaps". Perhaps rather than become too dejected at Showell's prognosis, we should marvel at the buildings of our land which did survive destruction.

The good Abbot Hockele was soon succeeded by a man of another temperament, Thomas de Pipe, who "in three short years commenced a very different career". We hear of him in 1365, granting away farms and lands for the support of his concubine, Isabel Beushale, and his children by her (which were more in number, so the record says, "than the monks in the Convent").

Through the Duke of Suffolk, the estate passed to Sir Rowland Hill (not the founder of the penny post but an opulent sixteenth-century London merchant) and, by marriage,

Blackdown Mill, a picturesque survivor now serving as the home of an antiques business.

to the benevolent Leighs. Showell wrote: "The estate has remained in the family ever since, and if all succeeding Leighs are as true noblemen as the present one, may it so remain as long as private ownership in land continues!" Let us hope this exhortation is heeded by modern Chancellors of the Exchequer.

Many acres of the lands of the Leigh estate are now occupied by the multiplicity of buildings and structures of the National Agricultural Centre. Each July, Stoneleigh is the mecca for thousands of farmers and other visitors from these islands and beyond, when the Royal Show is held.

Along the banks of the little River Sowe, I traced Showell's steps to its confluence with the Avon. The huge osier beds have become superflous with the ubiquitous plastic taking the place of willow shoots for baskets. Now there are tall plantations beside the river. The fine stone bridge which once carried travellers from the abbey to Kenilworth still stands, but now day-trippers cross it to find their picnic places in the park.

The Avon curves here around a wooded hill, so describing a perfect "S". I walked along the straight road (B4115), then took the turning which leads to nowhere but Ashow.

Showell credited the neatness and trimness of the place to its non-possession of a beer-house. "Happy Ashow" he called it, and obviously did not think an inn enhanced a village. I wonder what he would have made of the village club which occupies one of the old dwellings today.

Now Ashow is prosperous and prosperity brings neatness and some loss of what is inherent in an English village: the right "mix", not only of villagers but of architecture too.

The church tower just about tops the nearby yew. "The tree," we are told by Showell, "must be among the finest in any English churchyard." It is a reminder that the long bow, the most deadly of all medieval weapons, in the use of which our forbears were especially proficient, was made of yew.

In 1363, Edward III ordered the general practice of archery on Sundays and Holy Days. The practice often took place after worship and in the churchyard. At Ashow there is a rare survival in connection with this. The east wall of the chancel is deeply scored with marks made by the sharpening of arrows.

The Avon flows within a few yards of the church and here it speeds through the reeds in a deep channel. A pathway is carried high over the water on a footbridge, then continues through the flat fields of the valley to a road. Here, I turned right to Chesford Bridge which has to take the busy traffic of the A452 over our river. Seemingly as an antidote, the Avon is now languid and soothing; I watched the first yellow leaves of autumn drifting downstream towards Blackdown Mill.

Today the mill houses the business of an antiques dealer. Stone steps lead to the high galleries and creepers decorate the walls, but the wheel is unlikely to turn again.

Half a mile distant, is Leek Wootton – and Blacklow Hill, setting for a macabre episode in Warwickshire history. On the night of 1st July, 1312, Piers Gaveston, favourite of Edward II, was kidnapped and taken to Warwick Castle. While his captors were debating what should be done with him, his fate was sealed by someone saying: "You have caught the fox; if you let him go, you will have to hunt him again." So he was hurried off and beheaded on Blacklow Hill. The spot is marked by the inscription: "In the hollow of this rock was beheaded by barons lawless as himself, Piers Gaveston, Earl of Cornwall, the minion of a hateful king, in life and death a memorable instance of misrule".

Around wide sweeps below hillsides, the river soon tumbles over the weir of the mill at Guy's Cliffe. Beloved by artists and writers, among them David Cox and Ruskin, the setting is truly spectacular, with woodlands crowding on to the low stone building. The

*The so-called Saxon
Mill at Guy's Cliffe
near Warwick, a
haunt of artists and
writers.*

Guy's Cliffe House. The growth of vegetation around the ruin today, makes the picture more exciting but, at the same time, sadder.

timber balcony looks Swiss and meets the overhanging trees; eternally there is the sound of water; across the meadows the bells of Old Milverton Church can sometimes be heard. This is a paradise indeed.

The mill now houses a fashionable restaurant, and its preservation looks secure, which is more than can be said for the towering ruin a hundred yards downriver. This is Guy's Cliffe House. A modern description states that the "tropical" growth of vegetation around the ruin today makes the picture more exciting but, at the same time, sadder. The writer rightly condemns a society which would allow a house of such magnificence and history to fall into decay.

The story starts with the legendary hero, Guy of Warwick, in Athelstan's time. It is said he went on a pilgrimage, returning at the time of an invasion by the Danes, whose champion Colbrand was at Winchester, challenging any Saxon to mortal combat to decide if the Danes should retire, or Athelstan surrender. Guy took up the challenge. Killing his man, he set out afoot, and alone, for Warwick, where dwelt his beloved Phyllis. Having arrived at Warwick, he, for some reason, "solicited alms of the lady with other twelve poor men, and she knew him not; then he betook himself to a rocky place beside the river, where dwelt a holy man, and here hewed himself a cave, in which he lived a hermit. When he was dying, he sent a ring to his lady as a token, which she recognised, and hastened to close his dying eyes". Thus we have Guy's Cliffe, dating back to 929.

Richard Beauchamp founded a chantry here and rebuilt the tiny chapel in 1422-3. He is also credited with the rock carving of Guy.

The house whose wrecked skeleton we now see was built on the exciting clifftop site in 1751 in a pure Palladian style for a Mr. Greatheed. A fisherman told me that the only time anything is heard now of Guy's Cliffe House is when more lead is stolen. Perhaps the tragedy of Guy's Cliffe is the close proximity of Warwick; the historic county town has an overflowing abundance of architectural antiquities. So onward, like the river, to Warwick.

"Welcome to historic Warwick". Such is the notice on the outskirts of the capital of the lands of Arden. In so many aspects we are reminded of the importance of this county in the unfolding history of our land. It is some pleasant surprise that Warwick has still retained so much of antiquity, despite the pressures of industry, money and relentless traffic.

Many of the buildings are gems. Is there, for instance, a thoroughfare of finer black-and-white cottages than Mill Street anywhere in the land? I doubt it.

One important building survived a bare twenty-five years after Showell's tour. The Priory of St. Sepulchre is now only remembered in the name of a street and Warwick's Priory Park.

The Priory was the first of the order established in the kingdom, and was founded before 1135 by Henry de Newburgh, Earl of Warwick. After being put out of commission by Henry VIII, the lands went to Thomas Hawkins (whose son, we are told by Showell, "after squandering his patrimony, died in Fleet prison"). It would appear Hawkins made a habit (and a fortune) by buying odd lots of abbey and church lands – a land speculator who would surely have prospered today.

Hawkins had little use for the Priory and replaced it by "a very fair house" – a Tudor mansion of some elegance judging by the sketch made by our traveller. If you want to see what the priory house looks like today, you will have to travel over the seas to Richmond, Virginia. In 1927 an American numbered the stones and carted the lot off to re-erect the place in his homeland.

Like Showell, I started my promenade around Warwick at the West Gate. The thoroughfare was carved through a huge outcrop of rock – then surmounted by the

36

A splendid architectural group in Warwick. It includes the West Gate, surmounted by the Chapel of St. James, and (on the right) Lord Leycester's Hospital.

Chapel of St. James. There is a mention of this gate in 1129, and the rebuilt chapel dates from the early fourteenth century.

The splendid group of nearby buildings includes the Lord Leycester Hospital. It was formerly a mansion or college belonging to the Guilds of Holy Trinity and the Blessed Virgin and of St. George. In 1571 it was acquired by Elizabeth's favourite, Robert Dudley, Earl of Leicester, for "such poor and important persons as shall hereafter be maimed or hurt in the wars in the service of the Queen, her heirs and successors especially such as be under the leading of us (the Earl) or our heirs or the servants or tenants of us and our heirs, shall be preferred before all others". Then (and when Charles Showell made his record) there were twelve brethren and a master "who must be an ordinary preacher of God's word".

Now there are only six and a lay reader and the negative qualification "not to have five pounds a year of their own" (raised to £80 by the turn of the century) has now gone.

On the death of one of the brethren, his widow has, of course, to leave; a few years ago she was a recipient from a fund derived from visitors' tips. A jovial guide and brother told me that there were few tips today – in spite of the many wealthy visitors from foreign lands. The wives now go on the Council's waiting list when the brethren take up residence, in order to safeguard a future home.

Showell told us that the silver badges and buttons worn by the original brethren, with their names and date (1577) were still in use, save one, which was stolen. My guide showed me his bear and ragged staff badge with the name of the original owner many years ago on the reverse side.

Like the Lord Leycester Hospital, St. Mary's Church nearby looks little changed from Showell's sketches. The tall early eighteenth-century tower is a landmark seen for miles around. About half the church was destroyed in a great town fire in 1694; but we can see the excellence of the original structure in the Beauchamp Chapel whose sturdy fifteenth-century stones survived the conflagration.

Dugdale gives a graphic account of the building of the chapel and a copy of the contracts for the work; its cost was £2,481.4s.7d. Showell calculated its equivalent worth in 1900 was fifty thousand pounds. Would a million cover it today? I wonder. The contract provided "that glass for windows was to be glass from beyond the seas, and no glass of England".

The ancient Caesar's Tower, towering above Warwick's Mill Street, was built immediately after the Normans came.

The church was founded before the Conquest; Turchill, the Saxon, provided the land on the hilltop. It was repaired by Roger de Newburgh in 1123 and his magnificent Norman crypt survives as does his Charter.

The Beauchamp Chapel was started in 1443 and its beauty was fashioned over the next twenty-one years. Showell quotes from Bloxham's *Antiquities,* a reference book of the last century: "The chapel is a magnificent building in the very finest style of the fifteenth century. On descending under a magnificent door canopy, the splendid proportions of the chapel are seen at a glance. There are four stately monuments, that nearly in the centre being Earl Richard, the founder; west of it that of Ambrose Dudley, the good Earl of Warwick; that on the south, to Robert Dudley, Earl of Leicester, who continued to keep his worthless self in good company not only living but dead. The monument remaining is to his son who died young".

A byway called Tink-a-Tank, reminiscent of a Gilbertian song in *Trial by Jury,* takes us to St. John's House at the east end of the town; it was constructed on the site of a medieval "hospital" which provided casual lodging and refreshments to poor wayfarers, and more permanent help to the local poor and infirm. The present mansion was built by the Stoughton family early in the seventeenth century, and today serves as a museum.

Nearby, is the Eastgate surmounted by St. Peter's Chapel which was reconstructed in the reign of Henry VI. Today it is used by the girls of King's High School.

We find an unusual pillarbox by the old gateway, said to be one of only four in the country. It is from about 1850 and designed by Anthony Trollope.

The crowning glory of Warwick remains the castle, "the finest medieval castle in Britain". On its rocky plinth towering above the Avon, it is of such a unique character that a visit is an event not to be missed.

The ancient Caesar's Tower was built immediately after the Normans came, and rises some 106 feet; beneath it there is a dungeon cut out of the sandstone. Guy's Tower is a more modest 93 feet and is relatively modern – dating back as recently as 1394 to a design of Thomas Beauchamp. The portcullis still exists in the massive double gateway; from above, molten lead and missiles could once have been sent down on any besiegers.

Beyond the lawns in the castle grounds is a great mound made by Aethelfleda, the daughter of King Alfred the Great, in about the year 915. This was probably used by

The East Gate in Warwick. St. Peter's Chapel surmounting it is part of King's High School for Girls.

William the Conqueror and later by Henry de Beaumond, the first Norman Earl of Warwick, on which to build the castle keep.

Showell quoted much of the interesting early history of Warwick from the fifteenth-century chronicler, John Rous:

"The first record goes back to Gulbeline, a British King contemporaneous with Christ. It was then called Caerleon, and was devastated, and 'rebuilt by Caractacus, who made a Mannour house there for himself'. Again and again it went through the process of destruction and rebuilding, once by a British Prince called Guayr, who caused it to be called Caer Guayr; this at the time of King Arthur. Now appeared the first Earl, Arthgal; Morvidus follows, 'who slew a man in a duel, his opponent encountering him with a young tree pulled up by the Root, in Token whereof he and his successors bore a ragged staff of Silver in a sable shield for their cognisance'. Destruction again – followed by restoration by King Warrimand, who called it Warrawyk. Again destruction by the Danes, to be renewed by Aethelfleda, that brave daughter of a brave father.

"Much later the De Beauchamps held the title. They came from Elmley Castle, a lovely spot on the Bredon Hill, in Worcestershire; the castle is now completely demolished, save a few of the foundation stones. The title remained in this family until the time of Edward IV; William de Beauchamp, 1267, was the first Earl. We find, even at the early date, earls embarked in commercial undertakings; if not as chairmen of companies, they did so in other directions. This William had a pillory and tumbrel, which he trotted out once a week, value ten marks; then again, his son and successor actually took out a patent (they were getting thoroughly imbued with commercialism, and evidently liked it) to tax the people of Warwick – wonderful invention, was it not? I give a brief outline of his specification. 'Patent for levying a toll upon vendible commodities that should be brought into the town for 7 years to repair the walls of the town, renewable for another 3 years'. This valuable patent was handed down to his successor, who 'renewed it for another 7 years, whereupon the Merchants and tradesmen who brought their wares hither forsook the Market and the town languished,' whereupon the Earl, like a wise man, seeing he was killing the goose that laid the golden eggs (evidently the goose is an ancient bird), abandoned the tax, when Warwick again flourished. It was this Guy that Piers Gaveston indiscreetly called 'the black dog of Arden', which was remembered when his fate was discussed in the 'black dog's' kennel.

"Another Beauchamp got into disgrace with Richard II, and was banished to the Isle of Man. Afterwards a prisoner in the Tower, he was liberated by Henry IV in 1399. Then we have Richard Beauchamp, the hero of three reigns, Henry IV, V, VI. He was the champion of the tournament and the joust; but he was also a brilliant soldier. He it was who bequeathed money for the erection of the Beauchamp Chapel, in which his remains were to repose. He also provided funds for the saying of five thousand masses in all haste possible after his decease, also that three masses should be sung every day in the chapel so long as the world might endure. Moreover, he instructed his executors to get a quotation for one mass a day at Tewkesbury Abbey for the same liberal period. We may rest assured, if such forethought meets its proper reward, he is now handsomely provided for. His only son, Henry, died at the age of twenty-two. He was the fifteenth and last Beauchamp.

"The earldom now passed by marriage to that most ambitious of men, Richard Neville, who married one of his daughters to the Duke of Clarence, brother of King Edward IV of York. Being concerned in an insurrection, he was obliged to fly to France, where were Queen Margaret and her son Edward, the Lancastrian claimant to the throne, to whom he married another daughter. Thus he had connected himself to both the Houses of Lancaster and York. Returning to England, he perished at the Battle of Barnet, on Easter Sunday, 1471, his son-in-law, Clarence, having previously forsaken him and gone over to the King. On the very same day Margaret and her son landed at Plymouth, and three weeks afterwards the tragedy at Tewkesbury took place, and the poor prince's widow, a mere girl, had to marry her dead husband's murderer, Richard Hunchback. The other sister, Clarence's wife, died, some say by poison; while six years afterwards her husband was drowned in a butt of Malmsey, because he was in the way of the Hunchback; and her son was beheaded by the same nobleman. Truly a happy time!

"On the death of Richard Neville, Warwick was without an earl, the estate being divided between his two loving sons-in-law, Clarence and the Hunchback. It so remained for nearly fifty years, when John Dudley was created Earl by Edward VI, as being descended in a roundabout way from the Beauchamps. There were rumours of his base origin, but 'of person he was very comely and of a spirit highly aspiring', says Dugdale. (He might have added, 'and an unmitigated scoundrel'). He met a death on Tower Hill which was too good for him. Among his many side ambitions and rascalities, as apart from his larger game, was the ousting of the rightful Lord Dudley, of Dudley Castle, simply because his own name was Dudley, and the possession of such a title would add lustre to it, although he was not even connected with that family. He was the father of Robert, Earl of Leicester, who was a true chip of the old block. He it was who wrote his mistress Elizabeth, from Holland, that Queen Mary should be quietly poisoned. His brother Ambrose now Earl, but dying without issue, the title again lapsed, and became extinct.

"The estate passed into the hands of the Crown until James's time, when it was granted to Sir Fulke Greville, at which time Dugdale says of the castle, 'it was a very ruinous Thing, the strongest and newest part thereof being only made use of for the common jail of the County'. He was stabbed by his servant, in London, in 1628, and was succeeded by his cousin, Robert Greville. The castle had now to withstand a long siege by the Earl of Northampton, in 1642, on behalf of King Charles I, and was relieved by Lord Brooke, who hastened up after the Battle of Edge Hill. This was the Lord Brooke who was shot in the eye by Dumb Dyot from the tower of Lichfield Cathedral. His son Robert was singularly enough one of the six Lords deputed to offer the crown to Charles II. Francis Greville succeeded in 1722, and in 1759 the title of Earl of Warwick was bestowed upon him".

The castle was sold to Madame Tussaud's by Lord Brooke in 1978; he now lives in warmer climes over the Channel. Previous to the sale he controversially sold many treasures of the castle, including the famous Canalettos, two of which were acquired by the City of Birmingham.

The last walk of the town I invite you to take is along a street whose charming and perfectly proportioned buildings would make an exile sigh for his native land; wisps of blue smoke drift from the little cottages towards the castle battlements; wisteria climbs high to the eaves; residents grow those old fashioned perennials which delighted the gardeners of yesteryear – such is Bridge End.

Pathways downstream from Warwick are few, so I had to contend with juggernauts as I followed the road to Barford. Showell passed a large sheet of water here "on whose surface innumerable wild life were disporting". Now the water near the highway is all bullrushes and weeds, and the herons have moved elsewhere.

Barford Mill of old has gone, and the lazy waters, freed of their labour, now amble

*A street whose charming and perfectly proportioned buildings would
make an exile sigh for home . . . such is Bridge End, Warwick.*

towards the old roadbridge. The present Barford Mill is in the same family that once owned the demolished water mill. One of the hostelries of the village now bears the name of Joseph Arch; during Showell's day, he ardently championed the cause of the agricultural worker. I called at the tiny yellow-painted cottage which was his home in Church Street. The farm-workers' union still remembers him, and its members each year march along this way, I was told by the lady who now lives there.

The river next turns north to Sherbourne. The village is a stately house, an elegant and lonely church with a slender spire, and a few farmsteads.

Wasperton, the next Avon village, has come up in the world since the turn of the century. The cottages were then described as "poor and mean". "I should not care to live at Wasperton," said Showell. Now there are attractive houses and gardens and, of course, the little church designed by Sir Gilbert Scott – a contrast to his massive opulent Gothic structure of the Houses of Parliament.

The path goes over flat meadows and around the edges of gravel workings to emerge on a lane by Hampton Lucy Mill. The water still tumbles beneath the wooden building, but the miller's place adjoining has become a smart mansion.

Although Showell did not think the mill picturesque, he did admire the "charming" view of the village and the trees. Now the village has changed and many of the trees have succumbed to the killing Dutch elm disease.

Hampton Lucy Mill. The miller's house has now become a smart mansion.

Charlecote Park, once the home of the Lucys and now cherished by the National Trust. **Above** *The Gatehouse.* **Right** *The main entrance gates.*

43

A sweetly melancholy picture: the former church and rectory at Alveston.

The road skirts the National Trust's Charlecote Park, and the irregular wooden fence contains the famous deer. These fine antlered animals browse oblivious of the sight-seeing tourists on the Shakespeare circuit from nearby Stratford.

The visitors come in droves – through the fine gates which show the skill of the wrought iron craftsman – and they call at the house built by Sir Thomas Lucy in 1558, the year of the first Elizabeth's accession. Indeed, it is said the mansion was built in the shape of a letter E to flatter the queen. Capability Brown, when designing the vistas for the gardens, made good use of the Avon which twists a way through the grounds, being joined by the little River Dene on the way.

The Shakespeare connection is quite nebulous. The youthful poet is said to have stolen a deer on the estate; he was caught and punished by Sir Thomas Lucy. When completing *The Merry Wives of Windsor,* Shakespeare remembered the admonition and mockingly based the character of Mr. Justice Shallow on Sir Thomas. Shallow, we read, had a coat of a dozen white luces (fishes).

The next village is Alveston; the mill was a ruin in Showell's day, so I was not surprised to find little trace on the site. The ferry here only lives in the name of the inn.

A muddy track between high banks leads up from the river, and we soon see the old church at Alveston. All that remains of the building the Normans began is the chancel, but someone obviously takes care to keep the little place of worship in good order. There are headstones bending this way and that, overlooked by a timbered building that was once the vicarage. All this produces to the onlooker a sweetly melancholy picture, contrasting with the newer Victorian church nearby.

Look through the window of the old church and you will see a strange inexpert sculpture – this is the effigy of Nicholas Lane. It has been suggested that he was a Stratford moneylender, and it is known that he had a dispute with John Shakespeare (William's father) about a debt of his brother Henry who lived over the fields at Snitterfield.

Passing expensive houses which have the back boundaries of their gardens bordered by the river, we reach Stratford-upon-Avon near the fourteen arches of the Clopton Bridge.

Clopton Bridge at Stratford-upon-Avon. During the civil wars, part of the bridge was demolished for securing the county.

This was named after Sir Hugh Clopton and dates from about 1485, "whereas before there was only a Timber Bridge and no Casuey, so that the passage became very perilous upon the overflowing of that River". So wrote Dugdale.

During the Civil Wars "part of the bridge was demolished by command of the Parliament for securing the county and preventing the incursions of the Enemyes".

Facing us now is the Royal Shakespeare Theatre. Showell called the theatre "conspicuously obtrusive". What we see today is the building of 1932, which replaced the earlier theatre burned down in 1926. Although it has been harshly criticised over the years because the architect Elizabeth Scott refused to build in the style of the traditional "olde worlde" but typified instead the radical "Odeon" trend of the 'thirties, the bricks have weathered and the main concern today is the difficulty in obtaining a ticket during the annual Shakespeare season.

Stratford is tourists and Shakespeare of course. I was walking through in November's mists. Guest houses were still displaying "no vacancies" signs; fashionable and elegant stores were aiming their expensive pottery and clothes towards visitors from Japan and the United States.

The Shakespeare Birthplace in Henley Street still looks identical to Showell's sketch. Coachloads of tourists were being led through the place clutching their guidebooks, then gathering politely around their courier like a class of schoolchildren of days gone by. "Here, on April 23rd, 1564, was born William Shakespeare, son of John Shakespeare, woolstapler and glover" . . . a cluster of wide-eyed Japanese listened

Stratford-upon-Avon. Shakespeare's Birthplace in Henley Street looks almost identical to Showell's sketch.

Above and centre
*Stratford-upon-Avon:
the Guild Chapel.*

Below *Stratford-upon-
Avon: the Royal
Shakespeare Theatre. The
architect refused to build in
the style of the traditional
"olde worlde".*

intently. The precious tree from which the young William may have swung, was propped up like an arthritic grannie.

The Shakespeare business has, unfortunately, brought the ancillary tourist "attractions". I can accept the exhortation above W. H. Smith's bookshop, "Come and take choice of all my library and so beguile thy sorrow" (Titus Andronicus, Act IV Sc.1.); or the 350-year-old inn "where his fellow townsmen joined him for his favourite drink"; or "Julius Shaw, one of the executors to his will, lived here"; but although I find it difficult to associate the likes of a motor museum or a waxworks with the poet, I know they are popular tourist attractions.

New Place, which we see now, was the home of Thomas Nash, who married Shakespeare's grand-daughter. The old "New Place" was where, from 1597, the Bard lived for many years of his life and where he died; it is said by the historian, Dugdale, to have been built by Sir Hugh Clopton. Little of the original house remains, having been destroyed by the Reverend F. Gastrell in 1759 rather than pay rates on the empty property.

A little distance away is the Chapel of the Guild of the Holy Cross. Take the cars away from outside, and the place has hardly changed since Showell wrote about it in 1900. It was founded some time before 1269.

As with so many other lovely buildings of our land, decay and deterioration have necessitated urgent appeals for restoration funds. Shakespeare would have looked upon the chapel's square tower but not the famous frescoes painted about 1500. John Shakespeare, father of the dramatist, was obliged to supervise the defacement of these decorations while serving as Chamberlain to the Corporation of Stratford in 1563. Paintings were discovered under the whitewash in 1804, although others were lost to Showell by being under a gallery, and came to light in 1955 when the gallery was removed.

The adjoining Guild Hall is from 1417, a building which, in the nineteenth century, the local council used for its meetings. Above is the Grammar School where Shakespeare acquired the rudiments of education, and beyond is the long frontage of almshouses with overhangs. In all, it is a magnificent group of Tudor architecture.

The beacon of Stratford is the spire of Holy Trinity Church, a historic place of worship on a splendid site alongside the Avon. We can, like Charles Showell in 1900, still approach the porch along an avenue of lime trees. He said they were planted a century before.

The church is collegiate, although the college has long since disappeared. There are stones of many hues in the braced tower, indicating its heightening in the early fourteenth century. The spire was added by Hiorn (a builder from upstream Warwick) in 1763. Part of the nave is probably of the twelfth century. Leyland says "the church was renewed in buildinge by John de Stratforde in the beginning of the reign of Edward the 3rd".

Showell tells us that Washington Irving gained admission to the church by "fishing out old Edwards, the Sexton, and accompanying him home for the key". Showell paid sixpence to the verger "who is always in attendance (the modest sixpence is a coin much in requisition at Stratford)".

Today, we too pay a modest amount to enter the chancel and stand with the other pilgrims at Shakespeare's tomb.

The word "beautiful" is overworked, but here is a place truly worthy of that description, especially if the sunlight is glinting through the great clerestory windows.

Leaving the church and proceeding along the High Street, past the almshouses, grammar school, Guild Chapel and New Place, we note a beautiful specimen of a decorated half-timbered building – Harvard House. This is from 1596, and was built

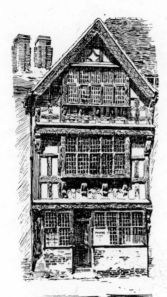

Above and above right
Stratford-upon-Avon. Harvard House in which lived the ancestors of the founder of the famous American university.

Right and below *Stratford-upon-Avon: the first lock on the river, with Holy Trinity Church on the far bank.*

AVONS FIRST LOCK.

ANNE HATHAWAYS COTTAGE

Shottery: Anne Hathaway's Cottage. The expanse of the nearby car park and coach area is indicative of the number of visitors from home and abroad.

following the major fires in the town of the previous two years.

It was erected by Thomas and Alice Rogers, whose daughter, Katharine, married Robert Harvard at Southwark in 1605. Their son John was born two years later and eventually journeyed to America. Although he only lived for twenty-nine years, his name is revered as the founder of the American university which was to bear his name.

Although we can see a treasure trove of Tudor buildings in Stratford today, there has not always been the same vigilance to preserve the town's heritage. "Even as I write," said Showell, "the work of demolition goes on."

A footpath over playing fields leads to the village of Shottery. Back in 1900 "octopus-like tentacles" were being extended by Stratford towards the village, and like Charles Showell, we have to contend with "the indications of civilisation undreamed of by Shakespeare." For us, these include a disused railway, barbed wire fencing and allotments.

But Shottery is pleasant enough with plenty of cottages of thatch, and roses tipping the roofs. Anne Hathaway's house attracts the tourists to Shottery, and the expanse of the car park and coach area is indicative of the number of visitors from home and abroad.

The Hathaway cottage still has the old-world flowers so often spurned by modern gardeners; externally, it is probably much as it was when the young William Shakespeare called to court the twenty-six-year-old Anne.

So it's back to the river, passing the theatre and church, to the site of Stratford Mill – "an ugly modern building", said Showell. Modern or not, it has now gone and is commemorated in the name of a block of flats.

The ruined lock that saddened our early traveller was reconstructed a few years ago, largely by the efforts of volunteers (including inmates of H.M. prisons), and it was possible to re-open the river passage from Stratford down to the confluence with the Severn. So, from now on, we will have the company of pleasure boats on our journey.

The navigation of the river was started in 1637 by a Fladbury man named William Sandys "who spent himself and the whole of his fortune in the work". Towards the end of the last century, the navigation was taken over by the Great Western Railway, which allowed its old rival to become abandoned and left to die.

There is a good riverside pathway, and the fishermen throng the waters. The rights are owned by the Birmingham Anglers Association – a wealthy co-operative and one of the largest fishing clubs in the land.

Just south of Stratford the volume of the Avon is swollen by the waters of the Stour, which contain the dissolved minerals of the Cotswold ridge from which they flow.

The next village is Luddington which lacks a centre, a shop or an inn. Few visit this place as no main highway passes through; but how different things might have been.

The present church is over a hundred years old, but many say that it was to the previous building that William Shakespeare brought his bride. Sadly, it is all conjecture as the ancient registers have been lost.

Weston comes next, then we reach the second Welford-on-Avon on our travels. It was a straggly village in 1900 – and is even more so now, with much that is modern to contrast with the old cottages of timber and thatch huddled around the church. But pride is here and by the lofty maypole is a notice that this was the best-kept Warwickshire village of 1977 "in the competition for places of over 500 souls".

Showell was upset by the fact that the church was "horribly marred by a coat of cement on the outside". This covering has now gone and the stones are honey-coloured and tinged with the look of the nearby Cotswolds.

Cleveland Green was the great benefactor of the village, but few remember now that the cottage on the green by the Bell Inn was once the gymnasium with "a circulating

Above and below left *Welford-on-Avon:*
cottages of timber and thatch huddled around the church.

Above right and below *Welford-on-Avon Mill.*
The river now passes by as though scorned.

library and other institutions calculated to give a man a taste for higher things than the pothouse kitchen . . . one penny a week constituting full membership".

The residents of Welford are well served by inns – the Bell Inn draws customers out from Birmingham with the smell of its curries; the Shakespeare Inn is sixteenth century, and by the river is the Four Alls, its name explained by the following verse:

The king who rules over all
The parson who prays for all
The soldier who fights for all
The farmer who pays for all.

The mill is still here and was working until a few years ago, but now it has been expensively converted into a house. The river passes by as though scorned, and the wheels of the machinery are garden ornaments.

A path keeps to a broad sweep of the river, and we see "haunted" Hillborough, a large gabled mansion of grey stone, lonely in a fertile valley just before we reach Bidford.

Showell said that there was much that is quaint and charming about Bidford, in spite of complaining about the old rural town being frequented by pleasure parties from Birmingham. The visitors still come, to enjoy the river, to learn of the village's historical associations and to marvel at the old byways and the cottages of great age. The old Falcon Inn still stands as solid as a Norman fortress; it was a dwelling house when our traveller was here at the beginning of the century, and is now the home of an antiques business. A long-awaited bypass is now in use, and the attractions of the village which were once threatened by the din and dust of continuous traffic, are now returning.

At the Falcon, we are told, the Bidford Sippers, members of a kind of convivial club, met their counterparts from Stratford, with Shakespeare among them, in a drinking contest. The Stratfordians were beaten off, and being unable to reach home, were forced to spend the night under a crab apple tree about a mile out of the town. In the morning, Shakespeare's companions urged him to return and renew the combat. He declined, saying he had had enough, having drunk with –

Piping Pebworth, Dancing Marston,
Haunted Hillborough, Hungry Grafton,
Dodging Exhall, Papist Wixford,
Beggarly Broom and Drunken Bidford.

Bidford-on-Avon's former Falcon Inn where Shakespeare is reputed to have taken part in a drinking contest.

The Romans took their Riknild Street to Bidford, and forded the Avon here. The ford was replaced by a bridge of eight well-proportioned arches back in the fifteenth century, and like so many of the Avon bridges, it is completely inadequate today.

The church of St. Laurence has a long nave, and much of the structure was rebuilt "during that fatal time, 1835". The tower has been overlooking Bidford for seven hundred years.

Over the bridge and by the recreation ground, a pathway cuts off a corner of the river, across the fields and stiles to the hamlet of Marlcliff – just a cottage or two below a wooded escarpment. We keep at the foot of the ridge to Cleeve Wharf.

Here, there once was the hustle of industry at the mill, although now not a stone remains. I climbed the lane out of Warwickshire into Worcestershire, and came to the village of Cleeve Prior on the hilltop.

Here, the Manor House, now the home of a farmer, is maintained with meticulous care. There are beds of wallflowers along the drive to the adjoining farm, and the blooms

Bidford-on-Avon. A ford was replaced by a bridge of eight well-proportioned arches in the fifteenth century.

are fringed by impeccable lawns. Overlooking it all, are trimmed yews cut into irregular arches, pillars and knobs, which give the place an inexpressible and rare charm.

The Manor House is said to have concealed Thomas Bushell in a hiding place in Stuart times; he supplied Charles I with money when the Royal Mint was in the hands of the Parliamentarians.

Passing the King's Arms Inn, where the walls are still perforated for pigeon holes and the welcome is warm, I neared the river again – then took the bridleway which starts at the edge of the escarpment of Cleeve Hill. This is a fine track, perhaps a Roman road. Numerous fragments of their handiwork have been unearthed from the cultivated fields nearby.

From this height we can look across the vale to Salford Priors. The church of St. Matthew demurely hides her tower behind the trees, but the most interesting building is a mile to the left at Abbots Salford. This is gabled Salford Hall, an Elizabethan building which was the seat of the Eystons – related to Sir Thomas More. It

Cleeve Prior: the trimmed yews of the Manor House give the place an inexpressible and rare charm.

Salford Priors: the gabled Salford Hall is Elizabethan and now a hotel.

subsequently found use as a nunnery, but the Roman Catholics of today worship in a tiny utilitarian building which resembles an ex-Army hutment.

At least Salford Hall is preserved. Showell found it fast going to decay and romanticised about the coming and going of the knights and dames of the courtly times of Elizabeth. There are comings and goings still, in our modern Elizabethan times, for the Hall is now a hotel and restaurant.

Downstream is Harvington, a village of typically Worcestershire black and white timbered cottages, set in orchards and peaceful now the main road is diverted. Harvington weir shows the strength of our once tranquil waterway; the river here is fifty yards across, and the waters tumble and chase down the slope.

Harvington Mill is nearby. The walls have a coat of dark green ivy, the roof is of rusty iron, the machinery has been plundered but the owner still hopes one day to restore water power once more.

Showell quotes from a pamphlet of a local historian, a Mr. Tomes: "The most casual inspection of the space around Harvington Mill will show that it has been raised by artificial means – probably at the time when the navigation was made about 1637 in Charles I's reign."

Harvington: the walls of the mill now have a coat of dark green ivy and the roof is of rusty iron.

At the end of the weir, foundations have been found of a more ancient mill, together with a mass of cinders, indicating that at an early period there was a furnace here for smelting iron.

Today, a modern lock has been built to take the holiday craft around the rapids.

At the B4510, I turned away from the Avon heights to the Littleton villages. Our traveller, at the turn of the century, came to Middle Littleton's St. Nicholas's Church and again complained of the recent (1871) restoration. "This," he said, "means that a building of Norman, Early English, Decorated and Perpendicular styles was destroyed. The whole of this beautiful valley appears to have suffered from this terrible scourge of restoration which swept over it with such virulence about this period, that it reminds one of the Black Death in East Anglia."

But Middle Littleton's pride is the huge tithe barn which nestles with the church and manor house. It was built by John de Ombersley, who was Abbot of Evesham from 1367 to 1377, and measures one-hundred-and-thirty feet long with a breadth of forty-two feet. The arches of the doorway are large enough to admit a wagon load of hay or corn pulled by four horses – which Showell assures us could be turned round inside the spacious building.

Middle Littleton's pride is the huge tithe barn which nestles with the church and manor house.

The buttresses have held up the four-feet-thick walls over the centuries; now the National Trust is the buttress. Craftsmen were working on the roof when I was here, carefully grading the grey limestone tiles, smallest at the ridge and largest at the eaves in the old Cotswold tradition. Cows grazed and gazed, oblivious of the history in their backyard.

A pathway over the meadows goes to South Littleton. The curious Dutch-looking house in the village, noted by Showell, is still here, and twelve dormer windows survey the scene. The building was deserted in Showell's day, then the army occupied it in the second world war; afterwards it was converted into a highly desirable residence.

The river, flowing generally in a southerly direction, twists sharply by the Fish and Anchor Inn for a short way to the north-west. The waters border the road here and there was once a ferry. The map tells us this is a fording place but on a stormy day in the late winter, the deep Avon mocks at this suggestion.

The Vale of the Avon now becomes the Vale of Evesham. This is market garden country providing for the larders and deep freezers of Britain. Past fields of onions and sprouts I walked to Offenham. An ancient place this, and it was twelve hundred years ago, when Offa was King of Mercia, that he established his headquarters here. In 1289, we learn, Edward I retired to Offenham in disgust, leaving the monks of Evesham "on account of their uncleanness".

Offenham Ferry is by an inn and provides a link across the river for the many anglers and the occasional rambler. A stream which tumbles down from the gentle slopes of Broadway Hill on the Cotswold fringe joins the Avon nearby. It's only a tiny brook, but our thrifty forefathers reckoned it could power Falke Mill. The mill has gone but the miller's house survives, and grindstones find a resting place in the garden.

With the winter sun now disappeared behind the hillsides of orchard trees, the air was chill and I hastened to the lights and warmth of Evesham to seek a room for the night.

★ ★ ★

The site of the Battle of Evesham is marked on the maps to the north of the town. It was on 4th August, 1265, that Simon de Montfort, Earl of Leicester, was caught in a trap with the river behind and on two sides of him, and the armies of Prince Edward, son of Henry III, in front. The old de Montfort, seeing his impossible situation, is said to have declared: "Now God have mercy on our souls, for our bodies are our enemies."

"No quarter for rebels," was Edward's command; and the Earl and all his men were cut down.

The history of this fascinating town goes back much further. About the year 700, Egwin was the Bishop of Worcester. He journeyed to Rome and made such a good impression that on his return the King gave him a large tract of forest land. Being fond of pork, this prelate kept pigs and employed a swineherd, Eoves by name. Thus we have Eoveshome or Evesham.

When Eoves told his master he had seen the Virgin, Egwin himself hastened to the spot and witnessed the sight. Egwin construed this as a command to build a monastery.

At the time of the Domesday Book the abbey possessed over twenty thousand acres. About 1319, it was remodelled and practically rebuilt. The last abbot was the most worthy Clement Lichfield, and he was embellishing the abbey in 1537, including the great Bell Tower, when Henry VIII started his dissolution of holy places such as this.

A hundred years later, Habington wrote a survey of Worcestershire and said: "Nothing remains but a huge heap of rubbish overgrown with grass". That's not quite true, as the glory of the Bell Tower (restored by the proud inhabitants of the town some years ago), can still be seen, and nearby is an archway to the former Chapter House.

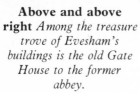

Above and above right *Among the treasure trove of Evesham's buildings is the old Gate House to the former abbey.*

Right and below *Evesham: the mill is now used as a social club.*

Evesham's mill still stands – at least the shell does – and is used as a social club.

There are two churches vying for attention near the Bell Tower. They were erected by the monks for the use of the inhabitants of the town. All Saints is from the twelfth century and St. Lawrence's a little later. It was in the latter church that Abbot Lichfield was laid to rest after his beloved abbey had been sacked on the orders of Henry VIII. Like so many of the heritage churches of our Avon walk, these require urgent funds to save them for the future.

Near the churches is Merstow Green where there are several interesting sights to see. The stocks were resited here after removal from the Town Hall jail in the 'twenties. The

Evesham: two churches stand near the old Bell Tower.

Evesham.

Hampton: the ferry is still well patronised.

Almonry Museum, once the abbey almonry of the late fourteenth century, now houses local antiquities and bygones.

Hurry across the main road when the procession of traffic stops, and look at the fine doorway, weatherstained and worn, of the workingmen's club. It once was the portal to the old grammar school which the noble Clement Lichfield endowed.

Walk along the High Street and the gem of the treasure trove of buildings is perhaps Booth House, otherwise the Round House, apparently so named because it was (and is) possible to walk right round it.

Beautifully restored by loving hands, it has jettied upper stories, and is now discreetly used as a bank. It was once an inn, and never a booth or market hall.

A few yards further – on the opposite side of the road – is Dresden House, dated 1692 on a rainpipe.

Bridge Street takes the busy A44 traffic over our river, and on the bridge we read the dedication: "To the public spirit and perseverance of Henry Wakeman are ascribed the origin and completion of this bridge" (in 1856).

Mr. Wakeman, a former mayor of Evesham, can also take credit for the tree-lined gardens which border the river so attractively.

Now there is a wide sweep of the Avon and we can see the tower of Hampton Church nestling in the trees. The ferry at Hampton is well patronised; it cannot be a gold mine with its low fares, but the rival bus to take the villagers to town is very much more expensive.

I took the high bridleway through orchards to Charlton and Fladbury. Showell is not precise on this route, but the points of interest are on the other bank and we get good views from our lofty track.

Just outside Evesham, we can see Abbey Manor. On this hillside the bloody Battle of Evesham took place, and fragments of the abbey were brought here when the ecclesiastical site was excavated early in the nineteenth century.

The hill continues for some distance, and in one hollow nestles the mansion of Wood Norton. When our traveller walked this way, it had just been completed by the Duc d'Orleans, banished from his homeland. Today the house is joined by alien modern buildings and is used by the British Broadcasting Corporation.

Chadbury Mill is a gem and would take my prize for the finest of any on the Avon. It is a tranquil retreat, and looking downriver to see the western sun setting is surely a sight of a heaven on earth.

*Chadbury: the mill is now transformed
into a private dwelling.*

Cropthorne: brown thatch and white walls still create a corner of Worcestershire which is everyone's idea of old England.

Above and right *Fladbury Mill – its machinery was turning from Domesday until as recently as 1930.*

Below and below right *Fladbury: there is no longer a ferry across the Avon at this point.*

Pershore, with its abbey dating back to 689.

Cropthorne and Fladbury are either side of the river, separated by barely a mile of waterway and the Jubilee Bridge ("cheap, nasty but useful", said Showell, but the one he was referring to was replaced in 1933).

Fladbury ("Fleodanbyrig" – a town by the river side) is an ancient place and was once of importance with a monastery. St. Egwin (who founded Evesham, you will recall) was here until 693, but when the Normans came, the monastery declined although it is recorded that a Convocation of Abbots was held in 1242 and the community received a royal visit from Edward I in 1291.

There are many buildings in Fladbury which make a pretty picture. The church is an edifice from the fifteenth century with well-preserved brasses of John Throckmorton and his lady, and cottages from past ages are gathered around the square. But the jewel of Fladbury remains the mill.

Loved by artists and fellow travellers who enjoy beautiful things, its machinery had been turning from Domesday until as recently as 1930. Now, like so many other mills on our way, the forceful water cocks a snook at hard work and escapes gleefully over the weir.

It is only in the last few years that the river has been made navigable again after centuries of neglect, but (as I have mentioned before) it was a Fladbury man (a Mr. Sandys) who first made the passage of craft possible, in the reign of Charles I.

So we walk the short distance downstream, then climb the wooded hillock to Cropthorne. Away from main roads, Cropthorne seems timeless. The Post Office may have moved to other premises from Showell's day, but brown thatch and white walls still create a corner of Worcestershire which is everyone's idea of old England.

The church is well maintained and we can see the Dineley monument (1624) which colourfully features effigies of Francis and his productive wife. No less than nineteen sons and daughters surround their parents.

Cropthorne's mill is a little way upstream opposite Fladbury, and presents a striking picture when seen across the river.

Through rather uninteresting and flat countryside, we come to the Avon's next mill at Wyre Piddle. The suffix is the name of the brook whose waters swell those of the Avon nearby.

Showell called Wyre Mill "the ugliest mill, of which Avon is ashamed" – which presumably does not please the members of the sailing club who use it as their club premises. No one can accuse the residents of the long Avon valley of not making a varied use of the old mill buildings. We can readily recall exclusive homesteads, clubhouses, an antiques business, a restaurant and so on. It's a pity though that not one is still used to grind corn.

A riverside path goes through the meadows where cattle graze, to the Georgian town of Pershore. This is a plum town if you visit it in late autumn, and it was once said that if a Pershore man was asked from whence he hails, his answer was governed by plums. If it was a good season, the answer was "Parshore surely" with an emphasis on the "ly"; in a bad year – and there have been plenty of late with lingering frosts – "Parshore, God help us!"

Pershore's joy is the great abbey, with a history dating back to 689 when a wooden building was established on the site. The timbers survived until a disastrous fire of 976, and then a similar fate befell the rebuilt abbey, and much of the town, in 1288.

The great tower which overlooks the town was re-erected in 1331 but the portion of the abbey west of the tower was never rebuilt.

Westminster Abbey was the beneficiary when much of the land of Pershore was seized by Edward the Confessor. This explains the close proximity of the former Church of St. Andrew which is within a few yards of the abbey. This was built for the

Pershore: the Church of St. Andrew,
built by the monks who were angered by
the loss of much of their land at the time
of Edward the Confessor. It is now used
as a community centre.

Pershore: the ancient bridge is now in
retirement, having been replaced by a
more modern structure.

Woollas Hall contains everything to help
romantic fancy.

people of Pershore by the monks who were angered by the loss of their lands. The church – now "licensed in pursuance of Act of Parliament for music, singing and dancing" – is used as a meeting place for the clubs and other organisations of the town.

The interior of the abbey has much of great beauty with a most excellent example of a fourteenth-century vaulted roof. The lines of the exterior are broken by massive flying buttresses, built to stop the abbey sinking in the soft soil. This strengthening dates from 1913.

As you stroll down the main street, glance at the decorative doorways – no two are alike – and each one is a reminder of the Georgian age of elegance.

Pershore Mill was at the west end of the town and perished in a fire in recent years.

The ancient bridge, built sturdily in the sixteenth century, is now in retirement and looks smugly at its more modern successor. There is a riverside path to Tiddesley Wood, and to the south is Bredon Hill, looking like a dormant sea creature crouching in the green sea of the Vale. As a local weather rhyme says:

When Bredon Hill puts on his hat
Ye men of the Vale, beware of that.

But on this day the air was clear and the bold outline was punctuated only by the undulation of the hillfort and the folly tower. The latter satisfied the whim of a Mr. Parson to raise Bredon to a height of one thousand feet.

The river, which has been coquetting with Bredon Hill for miles, now apparently makes straight for it. However, after skirting Great Comberton, the course sweeps gracefully to the west and soon emerges into an open valley.

Tiny villages such as Bricklehampton and the Combertons, are clustered around the base of Bredon like gems around a crown. Elmley Castle was termed by Showell as "an indescribably sweet village". Little has altered today, and the eternal brook still tumbles in a channel edged by lawns beside the main street.

After two sharp bends the Avon reaches the place marked on the map as Nafford. It's a lovely hamlet of a cottage or two, but those unsightly signs of civilisation were here – muddy car tracks where no vehicle ought to go, and filthy litter.

The Worcestershire Nature Trust has a reeded sanctuary where birds gather in the marshland, but there was no sign of the mill – just a few lumps of rubble overgrown with brambles, and that was it. I was going to make further enquiry but I was greeted by the warning "Beware of guard dogs" – then the hounds themselves – so I climbed to Woollas Hall, clasped in a hollow of Bredon Hill.

"One cannot", wrote our traveller of 1900, "long explore the house and wander about the grounds without becoming imbued with the spirit of nearly three centuries ago, and the place becomes peopled with Cavaliers and Roundheads. We can at once recall the troublous time of the Gunpowder Plot. We can see the horseman galloping over the lonely hillside, bringing tidings of the failure of the scheme, the consternation of the household, the closing of the secret entrance to the chapel – and the hasty preparations for flight. The Hall contains everything to help romantic fancy".

Today, there are shouts of children at play, for Woollas is divided into flats and – in contrast to many great houses on our travels – is alive and better for it.

From Woollas, a track twists a way to the summit of Bredon, and the climb earns the reward of a glorious panorama.

Showell wrote: "Facing us, after beginning like a table land, the hill slopes gently to the south, which in turn is bounded by that Chinese Wall-like range, the Cotswolds. On the north, a rolling country thickly timbered, from the midst of which stands out Pershore Tower: to the west and south-west the valleys of the Avon and Severn lie before us like a carpet, the Avon glinting in the sun in the most unexpected places".

One also recalls the words of A. E. Housman –

Above and below left *Eckington village, with its old church tower.*
Below right and far right *Eckington Bridge: the colours in the weathered sandstone still shine.*

In summertime on Bredon
The bells they sound so clear:
Round both the shires they ring them
In steeples far and near,
*A happy noise to hear.**

But we must end the rhapsodising and retrace our steps down the steep green slopes, back to the Vale.

The old road builders were frugal with their bridges over the river, and now the waters are some forty-five feet wide at Eckington Bridge. The stone parapets look as venerable as in Showell's sketch, but they now are braced with tie bars to bear the traffic of today. The colours in the weathered sandstone still shine – the rich greens, greys, yellows and deep reds.

Eckington village is topped by the old church tower. There is the curved masonry of the Normans, but the fine doorway is marred somewhat by the intrusion of an Early English window. On entering the church, look upwards: the simple carved oak roof was covered with plaster early in the last century, but Showell remarked that it had been removed "in recent times".

There is a brick wall bordering the churchyard – this once was the wall and oven-back of the village bakery. Now the premises are part of a garage, and it goes almost without saying that what Showell called "as fine a row of elms as may be seen anywhere" have long succumbed to the peril of Dutch elm disease.

*From *A Shropshire Lad* published by George G. Harrap.

Near Eckington: the mill house is now the dwelling of the lock-keeper.

The village has a good number of half-timbered and thatched cottages. The Post Office shares a shop which prominently announces that it is the local art and craft centre, an indication that Worcestershire weaving, pottery and reedwork find a ready market.

Over the railway – there was once a station here, but Dr. Beeching decreed it should go – there is a long lane to the river. This was a way to the mill of Eckington, but now there is a lock here and the keeper lives in the miller's house. Of the mill there is no trace, and it was deserted even at the turn of the century when Showell was here.

We can just see Strensham Mill in a copse to the left. The splendid isolated site ensured its continued existence as a house after its working days ceased. Strensham church is high on a ridge overlooking the Avon Valley, and just tops the trees. It contains brasses and monuments to the Russells – lords of the Manor in past days – and there is a tablet to the memory of Samuel Butler. He was born nearby in 1612 and wrote his poem *Hudibras* as a satire against the Puritans and the Commonwealth.

Another mile along the river is North Bredon Quay. Perhaps there was once commerce here, but today the banks are the headquarters of an exclusive sailing club.

A short lane climbs to the B4080 and Bredon's Norton. Time changes things slowly in this pretty Worcestershire village. "It has just a dash of the Tudor architecture so lavishly displayed at Broadway; fine examples of thatched roofs and farmyards, the like of which cannot be found in this or any other county," wrote Showell.

The gem is the Manor House, the arched gateway to which is dated 1585. Showell sketched this without the elegant wrought iron gate which now graces it, and which the present owner informed me was found at Ilmington, far away in south Warwickshire.

Bredons Norton. The gem is the Manor House, the arched gateway to which is dated 1585.

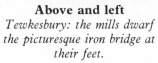

Above and left
Tewkesbury: the mills dwarf the picturesque iron bridge at their feet.

Below left and below
Tewkesbury: This end of the High Street has only changed superficially, and the gables of the House of the Golden Key still lean crazily.

Showell also described the old cider mill, but this is no more, except for its circular trough. New houses with a view now occupy the site opposite the Manor House. There is a huge barn nearby, but no longer is heard the sound of the hay wain and harvest. Instead, there is the applause of the villagers, for this is where Bredon's Norton's drama group performs.

But it is our next village where there is an even more spacious barn. This is Bredon, and the long stone tithe barn, like so many other buildings of past ages, is lovingly cared for by the National Trust. Extensive restoration work has resulted from a tragic fire in recent years.

The steeple of Bredon's fair church of St. Giles rises to 161 feet and is surely one of the loveliest in the Midlands. Masefield also knew of it . . . "All the land from Ludlow Town to Bredon's spire," he wrote. It was added to the earlier church during the days of wealth in the late fourteenth century.

With a sharp twist westwards under the M5 motorway, our river edges still closer to the Severn.

Twyning Green boasted the most southerly ferry of the Avon in 1900, but when I came here it was past history. I hailed a passing holiday cruiser to take me across to the inn – and into Gloucestershire.

"Do not fail to look back at Bredon," said Showell. "It is a fair scene on a fine June evening, with the setting sun glinting on the haycocks in the broad flat meadows."

Today, the rays are reflected in the windscreens of the incessantly passing vehicles on the obtrusive modern motorway. But the bold outline of Bredon Hill refuses to be excluded and brings man into a secondary and humble perspective to nature.

The pathway snuggles to the Avon over the lowland meadow, and the river's hasty dash to England's major waterway is now slowed. The final approach is gradual, hesitant and a little nervous.

The railway line no longer runs to Tewkesbury, and the remnant of its bridge over our river now attracts graffiti. There is the last major weir over which the river gaily tumbles, and the waters are divided into two for the last part of their journey. The so-called Old Avon cuts across the pasture of Severn Ham, and Mill Avon still has commercial work to do and slowly wends its way through Tewkesbury town.

The barges come up from Bristol docks bringing their cargoes of grain to the mills, which are tall, utilitarian and ugly, dwarfing the picturesque old iron bridge at their feet.

However, I have progressed too far along Mill Avon and we must retrace our steps to the road bridge – King John's Bridge – where the history of Tewkesbury begins.

The Bear – dated 1308 and Gloucestershire's oldest hostelry, it is claimed – is not many yards away at the corner of the High Street. This thoroughfare starts off with a sign of our modern times – a new shopping precinct that might well satisfy Birmingham, Bracknell or Billericay. It is an obtrusion in a country town of half-timbered buildings and old gables.

But sanity prevails further up the road, and the scene depicted by Showell, when compared with the same view today, has only the substitution of smart shoppers and motorcars for the yokel and cart. The gables of the House of the Golden Key still lean crazily; the Royal Hop Pole Hotel still courts trade by advertising that "this is where Mr. Pickwick and his friends stopped to dine, upon which occasion there was more bottled ale with some Madeira and some port besides, and here the case bottle was replenished for the fourth time".

Descriptions of the great buildings of our land are sometimes debased; superlatives abound and therefore tend to be of little relative meaning. However, can it be disputed that the great Abbey of Tewkesbury with its crowning glory of the Norman tower, is one of our finest structures? "It is beautiful in its massive simplicity," said Showell.

Tewkesbury: The Bear, Gloucestershire's
oldest hostelry, is just off King John's
Bridge.

Tewkesbury Abbey, with its crowning
glory of the Norman tower.

It did suffer, like so many other ecclesiastical establishments owning money and lands, at the Dissolution. The cloisters, Chapter House and Lady Chapel were destroyed by fire. How then did it not suffer the massive destruction wrought by the King's Commissioners on nearby Evesham? The good folk of Tewkesbury saved the church from Thomas Cromwell's clutches by acquiring the building by purchase. So we see today the Norman columns, each thirty feet high and twenty feet round, rising to simple arches and supporting the timbers of the fourteenth-century roof. The columns "look capable of carrying the roof for another eight hundred years, without the least fatigue", observed Showell.

There are tombs and effigies of the famous, the Abbots, the Dispencers, the de Briens and the infamous "false, fleeting perjured" Duke of Clarence who, in 1478, died in the Tower of London, drowned in a butt of Malmsey.

On the transept wall we can see a portrait of Mrs. Craik who set her book *John Halifax, Gentleman,* in Tewkesbury, calling the town Nortonbury. Opposite the Abbey gates, there is the Elizabethan Bell Inn, the house of Mrs. Craik's Phineas Fletcher, and nearby is his mill.

The wheel of our final mill has not turned since 1920, but the building is spruce and elegant. It belies its 700 years, and is now a fashionable restaurant.

Like the start of our jaunt, far, far away up in the hills of Naseby, the end of the river was once a place of bitter battle – this time the last great fight of the Wars of the Roses.

Queen Margaret of Anjou, wife of Henry VI and her son Prince Edward, landed at Plymouth in 1471. They were supporting Richard the Kingmaker, the father-in-law of the young Prince. On the very day of the Plymouth landing, Richard was slain at Barnet Field. So began Queen Margaret's forlorn march to Gloucester, a destination they were never to reach. On 23rd May, wrote the historian Holinshead, "about foure of the clocke in the afternoone, they came to Teukesburie, having travelled that night last past, and that daie, six and thirty long miles, in a foule countrie, all in lanes and stonie waies, betwixt woods without any good refreshing . . ."

The army was attacked by the King, Edward IV, in a field close by the town, known to this day as Bloody Meadow. Holinshead's description continues: "In a close, even land at the towne's end, having the towne and abbey at their backes; and directlie before them, and upon each side of them, they were defended with cumbersome lanes, deepe ditches, and manie hedges, beside hills and dales, so as the place seemed as noisome as might be to approach unto".

Tewkesbury: Bloody Meadow and the Council House – not the most attractive building my eyes had to behold on this Avon journey.

Tewkesbury: The last mill on the Avon was used by Mrs. Craik as a setting for Phineas Fletcher's Mill in John Halifax, Gentleman.

Today, the site of damp, willowed pastureland seems just as doleful and is made worse by the new Council House. It is not the most attractive building my eyes have had to behold on this Avon journey, and more suited to a film set for a remake of *Beau Geste*.

But to return to those days of long ago. Queen Margaret escaped across the Severn; the Prince fled into the town only to be handed over to the King. Edward demanded of the Prince "how he dared so presumptuouslie enter his realms, with banner displaied?" To this the reply came: "To recover my father's kingdom and heritage, from his father and grandfather to him, and from him, after him, to me lineally descended".

The King is said to have struck him across the face with his iron glove and the hacks, Clarence and Gloucester, pitiless, instantly murdered the boy.

★ ★ ★

Where Avon's friendly streams with Severn join
Great Tewkesbury's walls renown'd for trophies, shine,
And keep the sad remains with pious care,
Of noble souls, the honour of the war.

Camden's translation of Leland

The Avon, having silently witnessed the unfolding of the ceaseless history and development of our land on her travels through the heart of England, meanders on languidly. Then, as though tired and thankful to be at the end of her journeyings, slips, with scarcely a ripple, into the grateful arms of the Severn. Farewell old friend. . . .

Also from The Whitethorn Press . . .

Queer Folk
by Maurice Colbeck.
A comicality of Yorkshire characters.
£1.85. By post £2.10.

Yorkshire Laughter
by Maurice Colbeck.
A further comicality from the Broad Acres.
£1.85. By post £2.10.

Queer Goings On
by Maurice Colbeck.
Yet another Yorkshire comicality.
£1.85. By post £2.05.

Steam-up in Lancashire
Railwayana from *Lancashire Life*.
£1.00. By post £1.25.

Just Sithabod
Dialect verse from *Lancashire Life*.
£1.50. By post £1.65.

Cheyp at t'Price
More dialect verse from *Lancashire Life*.
£1.50. By post £1.65.

Flower Arrangement - Free Style
by Edith Brack.
£2.20. By post £2.45.

And, every month, the magazines:
Yorkshire Life
Cheshire Life
Lancashire Life
Gloucestershire & Avon Life
Warwickshire & Worcestershire Life

The Whitethorn Press Ltd., P.O. Box 237, Thomson House,
Withy Grove, Manchester M60 4BL.

The River Avon

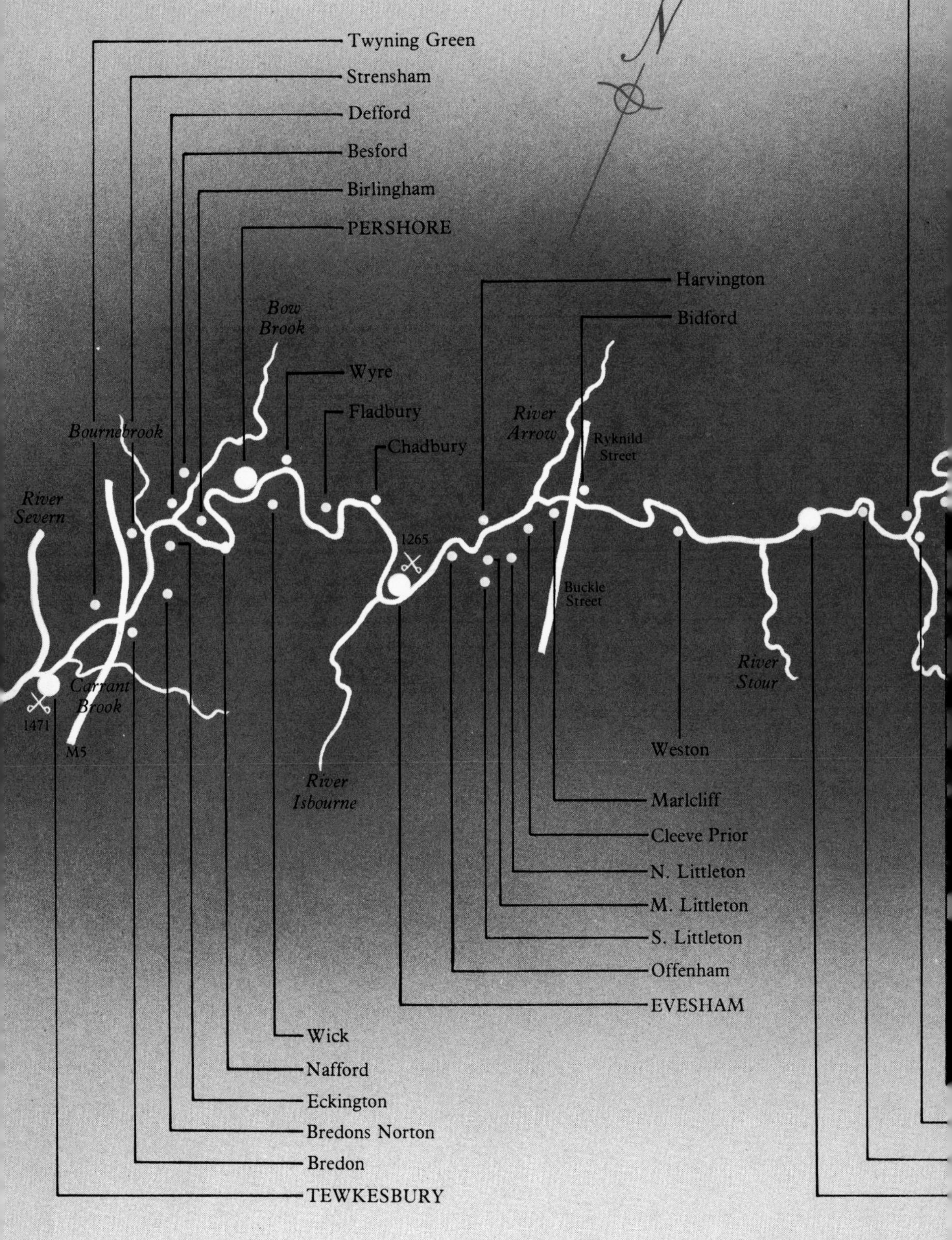

N

Twyning Green
Strensham
Defford
Besford
Birlingham
PERSHORE

Harvington
Bidford

Bow Brook

Wyre

Fladbury

Chadbury

River Arrow

Ryknild Street

Bournebrook

River Severn

1265

Buckle Street

River Stour

Carrant Brook

1471

M5

River Isbourne

Weston

Marlcliff
Cleeve Prior
N. Littleton
M. Littleton
S. Littleton
Offenham
EVESHAM

Wick
Nafford
Eckington
Bredons Norton
Bredon
TEWKESBURY

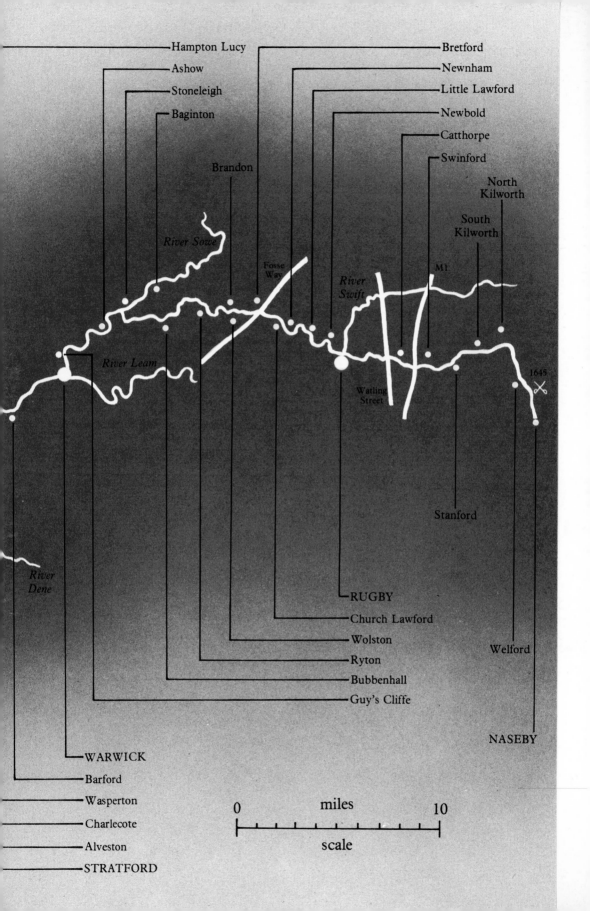

Hampton Lucy

Ashow

Stoneleigh

Baginton

Brandon

River Sowe

Fosse Way

River Swift

Bretford

Newnham

Little Lawford

Newbold

Catthorpe

Swinford

North Kilworth

South Kilworth

M1

River Leam

Watling Street

1645

River Dene

Stanford

RUGBY

Church Lawford

Wolston

Ryton

Bubbenhall

Guy's Cliffe

Welford

NASEBY

WARWICK

Barford

Wasperton

Charlecote

Alveston

STRATFORD

0   miles   10

scale